SCREAM
Southeast Asia
and the Dream

Scott Shaw

Buddha Rose Publications

SCREAM
Southeast Asia and the Dream
Copyright 1989 © Scott Shaw
www.scottshaw.com
All Rights Reserved

Front Cover painting by Scott Shaw
Rear Cover photograph by Hae Won Shin

First Edition 1989
Second Edition 2011

ISBN 10: 1-877792-01-2
ISBN 13: 978-1-877792-01-4

10 9 8 7 6 5 4 3 2 1

Printed in the United States of America

SCREAM
Southeast Asia and the Dream

1

awoke to a pounding rhythm
a movement
in a plastic vision
I wake to her asian eyes
staring into mine

> no,
> I don't want your love
> my head it hurts
> too much
> no,
> I don't need your love
> I can buy it anywhere
> on any street in town
>
> yes, I have compassion
> compassion for
> the fools
> yes, I made a promise
> a promise like
> all of those before
>
> words that means
> so little
> you can say anything
> and it will

mean nothing
my words
they are just the same

and tomorrow
it never comes
so don't talk about it to me
and today
it doesn't mean anything
I just don't want to
hear about it anymore

kiss me/love me/hold me
        let it last
        as long as it will last
        leave the promises
        for the family-men
        the businessmen
        the prophets
        and the preachers

        they have something
        to offer
        not me

give me cold hard love
cold hard cash
cold hard life
leading to
cold hard death
for that is where
all the promises go
anyway

a taste of the red wine
pour it into my glass
a kiss with your lips
if you please
      tickets to the passages
      into the sanctuary
      of the realms of the night

      lust,
      they say
      I look for lust
      I prefer to believe
      that I seek enlightenment
      worshipping
      the goddess
      who is bound
      by human form

and the waves of her body
pound onto me
like the surf
in the southeast asian sun
and her promises
they mean nothing to me

I listen
but words are all that I hear

so give me
my drug of choice
keep the speeches
for those who like to
listen to the lies
for me,
I know
that words
mean nothing
action speaks all
and what you can
show me
is worth more than
anything you could
say to me
please show me here,
with your body
yes, right there
place it upon mine

3

a dark kiss of victory
like the black curse
of the Goddess of Siam

black is the night
black like her hair
fading into a golden body
that melted into mine

      heat
      it pounds down
      upon me

      passion
      it dances on my soul
      and her love
      it lasted only a moment
      a moment
      well,
      that was long enough

4

I drink a glass of suicide
redemption in a cup
a lady she lays next to me
I do not know her name
      skin dark/hair black
      burned by the southeast
      asian sun

      and if I were
      any more than her
      or if the price,
      it was not so high
      then I would take her
      away with me
      run in any direction
      where the night
      would not hold our souls
      so bound

      but she and I
      no,
      we will never be given
      a second chance
      for destinies hold
      is far too tight
      so, I kiss her

one time for the moment
I kiss her
one time for the dream
I kiss her
one time
for no reason at all
I kiss her
and wonder why
life has let us go astray

so feed me what you have
to give me
I will take it
in any form that it comes
the night time it is for whispers
the day time it is for screams
spread your love disease
upon me
leave me
no room for escape

5

red wine touches my lips
her golden body touches my body
and the heat it pounds on my soul

a moment for the illusion
a moment cast only to the memory
and it was love that lasted forever
forever, it was only a day

the ceiling fan rotates
the vision of the sunlight in burma
is fading
the green flowered
wall papered walls
turn to gray

the fan turns
I turn
she turns

covered with sweat
our bodies merge
all rotates/as my head spins
as forever is only a moment
and the goddess
has once again stolen my soul

6

a bangkok morning screams to me
awoken by the chao praya ships
that move on the river below

her essence it cries out to me
wailing to wipe away her tears

but looking into her morning eyes
all I can see is a reason to leave
the heat, outside
the heat, inside
it never is cool here
never, never, never
this heat,
it is killing me

and when all the dreams
have been desired
and all the desires
have lived then died
and when the love
showed me no answers
then the only conclusion
is to walk away
just walk away
leave to nowhere/leave to nothing

nothing never means anything,
anyway

    no reason to return
    walk out into the heat
    the fierce heat/the pouring
    heat/the pounding heat
    like a rabid awakening
    screaming for the dream
    all there is here is the heat

    hot
    life here, it is so hot

7

I met her on an airplane
jakarta to singapore
first kiss on a beach
at sunset
down in old mexico

maybe I am just getting older
maybe it is
that I just don't care
maybe it is that
in my memory
she just looked better
maybe
I am just far too tainted
to get excited
about experiences such as these

so leave the sunset kisses
for the movies
leave the semi-babes
for those who like illusion
leave the first loves
for the children
just give me a drink
just give me the cold hard night

where a first kiss
is not the only kiss
and the word, no
never comes to mind

let me live
the southeast asian nights
where any dream is have-able
and anything that is wanted
is placed directly in my hand

8

a knock
in slices its way
through the silence
slowly I rise
in the casual
semi darkness
open my hotel room door
the city of hong kong pounds
to a thursday night time rhythm
the city/the night/the illusion
below

enter
older than I thought she would be
eyes, a bit wilder
than their chinese origin
should allow
    she steps in
    my meditation
    for the evening
    my vessel of love
    a passage to passion

    paid for
    like all relationships
    all good things

love
that is bought and sold

in-house/of-house masseuse
oh, promise me your love forever
tell me
that you will never go away

keep my robe on,
she says to me
as she pulls back
the blankets on the bed
and lays me down
upon clean white sheets

white, it is for saints
this room is for the sinner
paint it black, if you please

I
on my stomach
her hands
upon my back

through the hotel room robe
thin white line/thin white lies

as the questions of purpose
plays a song in my mind
an answer to seek/a need to fulfill
what is the actual
name of this game
are we going to get down to it
or what

      she turns me over
      her eyes find their way
      to my pleasure zone
      as my semi exposed body
      is revealed

a notice of her glance/a smile
from her lips
her hands again moving
everywhere to nowhere

and like the perfect
paid for passion
like, how could I keep it down
hands placed
oh so precisely/move me
into the mood
the juices
they get a-flowing/the river rising

a promise/the price
it moves up, $700.00 US
and like all of the best
who get you where you want to be
and then later tell you the cost
it could only be paid
for what is money for anyway

        she raises her
        white surgical steel dress
        like a nurse/like a nun

        before I could even think
        say a word
        it was in/she was on
        on to off
        and all the purposes
        in between

leave it to some uncensored poet
leave it to your dreams

her body wasn't all in full view
the way I like it
I mean, I generally like to see
what I'm having

my vision was blocked
but I rolled her over
and for a second
it was in sight/insight
and for all the perfection
of this/of that pagan moment
I could not help
but fall in love

the dirty deed done
off and on her way out
she went

come again tomorrow, I said
but I never saw her again

and for all of those possible loves
that you glance at
see for only a passing moment
wished for
but they are gone
and never seen again

for all those dreams
that you only wish
could have happened

a paid price
is worth it all
to taste/to touch/to feel

and love, it is so easy
stabbed down deep
like a knife
in the heart
a meditation
it leads to enlightenment
mine
was complete that night

9

hotel wall painted off white
love wrapped in the arms
of strangers
call it a fool's passion
a promise for a price
      for when you want to play
      you know
      that you have got to pay

      the dreams spin
      plastered hard
      against an off white wall
            as the ceiling fan turns
            as we turn
            as the earth turns
            all counter clockwise
            and the nights
            live on forever
            screaming
            for the dream

a promised passion/a promised
price
and love,
what does it mean anyway

so hand me the lies
that out live the truths
give me an illusion
to hold onto
      and when
      the greatest illusion
      is seen to be
      that there is
      no illusion at all
      then the Buddha
      will have been
      understood
      and life, it will tick on

tick-tock
fuck the clock

10

the night cries of mystery
it screams for the dream
the day
all it does is whisper
far too silent/far too soft
in the wisdom
it is trying to convey

    and the sun bleeds
    its warm presence
    onto me
    awaking the dawn

        from one side/
        to the other side
        let me know its name

and all the wizards, they lie
and the sorcerers, they cry
and the holy,
they know nothing at all
for their knowledge
it is lost
in what is/in what has to be
what it is/what it ain't

and as for the sinners
they are the knowers

    sin, from the ancient
    hebrew, meaning to merge

dish me up a plate of illusion
for I have nothing left to lose
kiss me
with the lips of desire
a goddess in any form
give me a night
to experience truth
give me a night
of the kind
the holy will never know

hand me a cup of redemption
     suicide in a glass
let me live among those who know
the knowledge of the night

11

night time falls
as it tends to do
love
she wants to give hers to me

the light is dim
long black hair falling
it caresses my face
I look up
see her closed asian eyes
as her wet lips meet mine

I have to re-close my eyes
for it is all too much
like a fucking movie

kiss me/love me
yeah, sure
but let's leave all this melodrama
for the soap operas upon the screen
I prefer it raw
I prefer it hard

dirty and blatant
no prisoners taken
none looked for

then what is known
is known
what is felt
is felt
and the romance
it is left for the dreamers
who believe in all that bullshit

12

come over here
for I am tired
lay in my arms
lay upon my couch
let your asian eyes
look into mine
and talk to me of love
talk to me of marriage
talk to me of all of those things
that do not mean anything
no nothing, at all
lay w/ me
love w/ me
kiss me good night

13

a longing child like face
of abstinence
a glance back over the shoulder
I left without wanting to leave
love/time
it is all gone

       the stories they have all
       been told
       see them upon any
       T.V./movie screen
       but the love in the heart
       the knife in the stomach
       it is what has meaning
       not the momentary dreams
       of actors who lie
       some distant place/some
       distant scene

       there I was walking
       there she was standing
       her black hair
       blowing in the wind
       her asian eyes transfixed
       upon my soul

and the sun
sheds its light onto me
as the lies spun in my mind
and the gods
they offered me no answer
to the question
"do you still love me?"
as I walked away

I had no answer
I just walked away

letter from thailand
"won't you come back to me."
come back/go back
it never seems to be the same

now, I could go there
lay in her asian arms
do nothing but let the days pass
the nights scream
and live in the poetry

but going back
it's just like it sounds
it doesn't mean
or add up
        to anything

I've tried it before
even with her
but the memory
is always better
than the cold pagan cut
of the knife of life

the truth is bought
the lies come out

and all the words of love
didn't mean anything at all

so thanks
but no thanks
next time I'm there
I will just look the other way

15

disco dolly for rent/for hire
southeast asia
by geographical bounds
white lies/white eyes
it buys me an easy ticket
      into paradise

wet my lips
the drink does flow
beauty condensed
in an alcoholic form

skin so golden/hair so black
in her eyes
I see a green card/a dollar sign
my two tickets
to promised passion
in the burning heat of this night

leave the vows
for the fools who call themselves
the family men
I prefer this
      a different dream
      with every passing passion

a different chance
in every dance

a lie
it equals
all that I can take
a lie
and I never
need to speak a word

the dream night princesses
they simply apply for it
the color of my skin,
my hair/my eyes of blue

the night air is warm
in the radio station
and we are left alone
the music,
we place it on tape
to be played tomorrow

      tomorrow is always
      another day

so we sit back, she and I
and we dog down

peachy is her name
the princess of bangkok radio
pichitra on her U.S, passport
      named by the queen
      of thailand
        no lie

but now she has
developed a passion
it is a unbreakable spell
it leads her
from one day to the next

pong kow as it is called
      powder white

one minute spreads to the other
for soon she must be home
children to take care of
a Thai husband
who she doesn't love to love
but for now
the moment is simple
a time in which
I watch her eyes spin

      her eyes spin/my eyes spin
      an embrace in illusion
      an embrace of the best kind
      as she reveals to me
      all of her secrets
      and all of the powers of the
      powder white

here and now
it is all that matters
bangkok radio
simply pays the bills
the bills for a white princess
in a golden land

whose desire of illusion
sends her into the best
of what bangkok
has to offer
        white power ma

hello bangkok
this is your nighttime D.J.
rock'n hollywood scott
and my good friend peachy
tells me
that we are going
to pick up the pace here a little bit
with a band from my home town
of L.A.
but remember bangkok
when you wanta' play
you gotta' pay

a man, a bangkok man
stands
he stands hanging one
on the side of the deserting street

a lady, a bangkok lady
she is waiting/awaiting something
I know not what

the neon lights reflect
in both of their skins
      displaying/decaying
      telling a story
      that can never be fathomed
      never truly be understood

      only seen/only witnessed

he is dressed in gray pants
a dark blue shirt
his eyes are hidden
deeply into the pole

she has long black hair
a long yellow dress

and stares into some distance
that my western eyes
can never see

    I pass him/I pass her

    he is vacant
    his back turned to me

    her face
    radiates the reflecting colors
    pink/red/blue
    all of the bangkok night

him, I have no feeling for
her, I could love
if given the chance

    pictures and scenes
    and all the figures
    in a dream

they all add up
to the same thing
    nothing
    not anything at all

18

scalded by the heat
of the bangkok night
touched once too hard
once too often
and love
it proved nothing to me
     loved/lost
     loved again
but lust handed me the illusion
a dream worth living forever

     and so few could know her
     as I have known her
     goddess green
     bangkok night

and so few could have lived her
like I have loved her
     siam dream
     buddha gold
and all being had/all being held

     I run from her/
     I run back to her
     the price, my soul
     a price so high...

Scott Shaw is a prolific author, actor, filmmaker, and musician. Throughout his life Shaw has continually returned to Asia, documenting obscure aspects of Asian culture in words and on film. He is a frequently featured contributor to Martial and Meditative Art Journals and is the author of numerous books on Modern Literature, Poetry, Asian Culture, the Martial Arts, Zen Buddhism, Yoga, and Meditation.

Scott Shaw's
Books-In-Print include:

The Little Book of Yoga Breathing,
Nirvana in a Nutshell,
About Peace:
> 108 Ways to Be At Peace
> When Things Are Out of
> Control,

Zen O'clock: Time To Be,
The Tao of Self Defense,
Samurai Zen,
The Ki Process: Korean Secrets
> for Cultivating Dynamic
> Energy,

The Warrior is Silent:
> Martial Arts
> and the Spiritual Path,

Hapkido:
> The Korean Art of
> Self Defense,

Hapkido: Essays on Self-Defense,
Taekwondo Basics,
Advanced Taekwondo,
Chi Kung For Beginners,
Mastering Health:
> The A to Z of Chi Kung,

Cambodia Refugees
> in Long Beach, California,

China Deep,
Essence: The Zen of Everything,
Shanghai Whispers
Shanghai Screams,
Shattered Thoughts,
Junk: The Back Streets of Bangkok,
The Passionate Kiss of Illusion,
TKO: Lost Nights in Tokyo,
Bangkok and the Nights
of Drunken Stupor
No Kisses for the Sinner
Zen Buddhism:
The Pathway to Nirvana,
Zen: Tales from the Journey,
Zen in the Blink of an Eye,
Yoga: A Spiritual Guidebook,
Marguerite Duras
and Charles Bukowski:
The Yin and Yang of Modern
Erotic Literature.

www.ingramcontent.com/pod-product-compliance
Lightning Source LLC
Chambersburg PA
CBHW060428090426
42734CB00011B/2495